21st
Century
Skills Library

REMOTE SYSTEMS CONTROL ENGINEER

MATT MULLINS

Published in the United States of America by
Cherry Lake Publishing, Ann Arbor, Michigan
www.cherrylakepublishing.com

Content Adviser
Gordon Parker, PhD, John and Cathi Drake Chair of Mechanical Engineering, Michigan
Technological University, Houghton, Michigan

Photo Credits: Cover and pages 1 and 12, NASA/Bill Ingalls; pages 4 and 6,
NASA/JPL-Caltech; page 7, DoD photo by Petty Officer 2nd Class Gary Granger Jr.,
U.S. Navy; page 8, ©majeczka/Shutterstock, Inc.; page 11, ©Press Association via
AP Images; page 14, ©Dainis Derics/Shutterstock, Inc.; page 17, ©Yuri Arcurs/
Shutterstock, Inc.; page 18, ©iStockphoto.com/lisapics; page 20, ©AP Photo/
Damian Dovarganes; page 21, ©Istockphoto.com/mikkelwilliam; page 22, ©Naum
Chayer/Alamy; page 24, ©Kip Evans/Alamy; page 27, NASA/Ames/JPL-Caltech.

**Cataloging-in-Publication data is available from the Library of
Congress.**
978-1-62431-006-5 (lib. bdg.)
978-1-62431-030-0 (pbk.)
978-1-62431-054-6 (e-book)

Cherry Lake Publishing would like to acknowledge
the work of The Partnership for 21st Century Skills.
Please visit *www.21stcenturyskills.org* for more information.

Printed in the United States of America
Corporate Graphics Inc.
January 2013
CLSP12

TABLE OF CONTENTS

CHAPTER ONE
CONTROLLING THINGS FROM A DISTANCE

On August 5, 2012, the National Aeronautics and Space Administration (NASA) landed a robotic

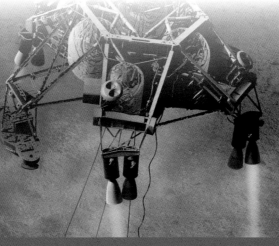

Curiosity's *landing was carefully designed to protect the rover from damage.*

six-wheeled truck on the planet Mars. The name of this moving laboratory, or rover, is *Curiosity*. It had traveled to Mars on a spaceship that looked like a flying saucer.

When the spaceship neared the surface of the planet, it came apart. A rocket-powered ship holding *Curiosity* dropped out. This device lowered *Curiosity* to the ground using cables. When the rover was on the ground, tiny explosives blew up and cut the cable lines. The rocket-powered ship then flew off and crashed nearby.

It was time for *Curiosity* to get to work. But first, the roving laboratory needed someone to tell it what to do. That's when specially trained **engineers** stepped in to give *Curiosity* its orders. Each morning, they provide the rover with its work schedule—from planet Earth, an average of about 140 million miles (225 million kilometers) away! The engineers send *Curiosity* its directions with radio signals. It takes about 14 minutes for a signal from Earth to reach the rover and another 14 minutes for one to come back.

The men and women who operate or **access** objects from a distance are called **remote systems** control engineers. It's a brand-new category of job titles, and it includes a lot more than communicating with objects in space. *Remote* means that these engineers work from somewhere away from the object they control. *Systems* describes complicated sets of tools and ways to use the tools. *Curiosity*, for example, is fitted with cameras for photographing the landscape of Mars.

It also has a long robotic arm that can collect samples of rock and soil. It is equipped with a laser to heat and analyze rocks. A **nuclear**-powered battery provides the energy needed to perform these tasks.

Remote systems control engineers work on a wide variety of important projects. Remote systems are often designed to

The rover Curiosity is equipped with tools to help it search for possible life on Mars.

The military uses remotely controlled robots to inspect possible bombs, with the controller standing a safe distance away.

be used in places that are unsafe for people, such as inside a nuclear power reactor. Some remote systems engineers operate machines that handle **toxic**, or poisonous, waste. They can also be used to handle dangerous chemicals. Some are used in warfare. These engineers might control robots that inspect possible bombs. Others fly drones, or unmanned planes. The drones fly over enemy-controlled or other dangerous areas while the drone pilots are miles away.

Remote systems, however, aren't used only in dangerous conditions. Wind turbines—huge, towering propellers you may have seen lined up in the countryside—are remotely controlled, often from great distances. The turbines change the energy of the wind into energy that can be used to produce electricity, power machines, or charge large batteries. Not only can the turbines be controlled from a distance, but engineers have also developed a remote-controlled robot that can inspect them. These robots are equipped with a camera

Remote systems help make jobs such as controlling and inspecting wind turbines safer and easier.

and are capable of climbing straight up 300-foot (91-meter) turbine poles without slipping off. The camera photographs the turbines and immediately sends back the images to the remote-control operator—wherever he or she may be!

21ST CENTURY CONTENT

Technicians who assembled and tested the *Curiosity* rover wore "bunny suits" of white coveralls, face masks, and booties to prevent Earth germs from hitching a ride on *Curiosity* to Mars. *Curiosity's* control engineers on Earth, however, can dress more conventionally: in slacks, collared shirts, sports jackets, and comfortable shoes. The control engineers work on Mars time, which means that every day, they report to work 37 minutes later than the day before. They do this to keep on track with the Martian day, which is a little longer than a day on Earth. Mars spins on its axis in 24 hours and 37 minutes. Earth makes a full spin in 24 hours.

Computers often use remote systems. You may have heard of **cloud computing**. In cloud computing, information is not stored in your computer. Instead, it is stored in remote places called clouds, which are part of the Internet. (The term *cloud* comes from the puffy, cloudlike shape that is often used to represent the Internet.) Cloud computing takes the work off your computer, so that it doesn't become overwhelmed with too much **data**. By using cloud computing, for example, large companies with hundreds or thousands of employees do not have to equip each worker's computer with the **programs** needed for the job. Employees can simply log into one database that contains the programs they need, thereby saving space on their own computers.

Doctors use remote systems that allow them to perform surgeries from hundreds of miles away from the actual patient. Suppose a person in California wishes to donate a kidney to help someone who desperately needs one. Amazingly, a doctor in Texas—or anywhere in the world—can perform the operation to remove that person's kidney. The patient lies in an operating room that is equipped with a surgical robot and video cameras. From his or her office far away, the doctor looks at the screen and operates the robot's arms to safely perform the surgery.

The cutting-edge, high-tech advancements being made in remote systems technology are almost impossible to keep up with. And the need for qualified control engineers is growing just as rapidly. Are you up to the challenge?

The first remote operation on a person's heart was completed by Dr. Andre Ng in 2010.

CHAPTER TWO
WORKING AS A REMOTE SYSTEMS CONTROL ENGINEER

The engineers who operate *Curiosity* have an unusual workday. They begin their day in a dark room full of

Rover engineers and scientists control **Curiosity** *from the Jet Propulsion Laboratory control center, also called the Dark Room.*

computers. They wear 3-D glasses to see what *Curiosity* sees. Then they write the computer programs that will instruct the rover what to do. They send this information in the form of radio waves across millions of miles of space. Fourteen minutes later, *Curiosity* receives its instructions and begins its work. Sometimes the engineers don't know how the rover's day went until they come back to work the next day!

Not all remote systems control engineers explore space with robots. Todd Assentoa is an engineer who works with cloud computer systems. Cloud systems use large information storage machines to save the valuable information of many companies. These companies pay Todd's employer to protect and copy their information.

The company Todd works for is called EMC. EMC stores information in large machines called **arrays** and backs up, or copies, data for its clients. If one of EMC's clients loses data, EMC finds it for them. EMC's clients include some of the biggest technology companies in the world. The Internet's largest retail company and auction house are EMC clients. Another client is the most popular online social media company. EMC also works with banks, hospitals, and even the U.S. Army.

But why would a company pay to have its data stored in a cloud? Many companies have too much information to keep on their own computers. Others just want to be very careful. A fire or flood can damage information storage devices. If there's a power failure at a business, important information can be lost. Cloud computing removes this danger. The cloud is a place where you can safely keep copies of all your information. The cloud is running all the time. It never turns off.

A job in cloud computer systems can include a bit of detective work.

When one of EMC's cloud customers can't get to its data, Todd springs into action. He'll contact the customer that is having the problem and sit at his computer to figure it out.

Today, Todd is speaking with a customer who works in a hospital in Canada. Todd listens to the customer explain the problem. It seems that one of the surgeons can't find important X-rays that have been stored on the hospital computers and that should have been copied on the cloud. Todd goes into detective mode. He connects his computer to the hospital's computer—thousands of miles away—and he, too, is unable to find the X-rays. Then he connects to EMC's arrays to track down copies of the missing X-rays.

Most of the time, Todd can solve the problem from his computer. This is usually the case when there are problems with the **software**, and something has gone wrong with the instructions the computers are using. Occasionally, Todd finds something wrong with an array. When he does, he sends a technician to the array to fix it. This is a **hardware** problem. It's a problem with the data storage machine itself.

Todd handles several of these types of problems each day. He also trains other engineers who are new to this kind of work. He observes them while they speak to clients and suggests ways to help them work more closely with EMC's customers. He also teaches them to be critical thinkers and how to respond to emergencies quickly.

Todd enjoys his work, especially the detective portion of it. He likes to figure out what's causing problems and discover clever ways to solve them. He also enjoys helping other engineers learn their jobs. He loves teaching. In his work on remote systems, Todd gets to be a detective *and* a teacher!

LEARNING & INNOVATION SKILLS

Until the early 1980s, very few people had cell phones. Almost all phones at that time used wires to operate. Back then, people couldn't watch movies, read books, or send text messages on their phones. Ask your parents what phones were like when they were your age. Try to imagine what phones will be like when you're the same age as your parents are now. How do you think you'll communicate with friends when you're an adult?

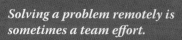
Solving a problem remotely is sometimes a team effort.

CHAPTER THREE
BECOMING A REMOTE SYSTEMS CONTROL ENGINEER

Remote systems control is a relatively new way to work. Most of these types of jobs have not been around very

Science and math skills are helpful for future remote systems control engineers.

long, and not all people who work as remote systems control engineers got their jobs the same way.

Todd went to college and studied psychology. He studied the way groups of people behave, and he learned how the human brain works. He also learned how people develop and mature emotionally. When he finished college, however, he had difficulty finding a job. He decided he needed to make a career change, and he began to take classes that taught him how to fix computers. After months of training and hard work, he landed his job at EMC.

"When I first went to college," Todd says, "I wanted to be a police investigator. Now I think of myself as an investigator for computers." He also thought about becoming a professor, because he always wanted to teach. Now he does both!

The engineers at NASA who operate *Curiosity* also came to their work in surprising ways. The head engineer for *Curiosity* is a man named Brian Cooper. He studied robotic vehicles. But another engineer who works with him was an artist. He was good at creating computer **animation**. Another one of the engineers majored in anthropology, the study of cultures and human behavior.

Even though they focused on different subjects, these engineers did have one thing in common: they were good at using computers. Some studied computer technology. Others just used computers a lot in their schoolwork and training. If you want to operate remote systems someday, you'll need to work with computers, too. And the more you use computers, the better you'll become with them.

Some of the rover engineers enjoy playing video games. Many researchers believe that some types of games, such as ones that feature virtual worlds, can be great learning tools. When you explore a virtual world, you're taking on the role of a scientist or an engineer facing a problem. You have to explore, perform certain tasks, and solve the problem. These

Computers are essential to the rover engineers and other people working with Curiosity.

Puzzle games and other video games can improve a player's problem-solving skills.

activities are very similar to the ones that rover operators carry out each day.

■ ■ ■

Almost all remote systems engineers work in science- and math-related jobs. Some engineers are scientists them- selves. Learn as much as you can about the different fields of science and math. The knowledge you pick up will be very helpful in your career as a remote systems engineer.

You can also visit science museums, especially ones that focus on technology. Many feature hands-on, **interactive**

Interactive exhibits give visitors a chance to experience hands-on science.

exhibits where you can learn about the latest developments in the field. If you're interested in space, check out an observatory, where scientists use giant telescopes to look into the skies.

There are many ways to prepare for work as a remote systems control engineer. You just have to get as much experience with computers as you can and soak up as much science and math as possible. Maybe you can one day turn what you love into a job like Todd and Brian did.

LIFE & CAREER SKILLS

Many engineers and scientists have fun jobs. They got their jobs mainly because they worked hard at studying a type of science that interested them when they were young. If you like rocks, read about geology, the science of Earth's physical structure. If the ocean interests you, study marine biology, the science of ocean life. Perhaps flying appeals to you. If so, check out some books about physics, the science that deals with matter and energy. There's a kind of science devoted to just about any subject—dinosaurs, water, weather, and much, much more. What things interest you? Can you think of what kind of scientist studies that?

CHAPTER FOUR

THE FUTURE OF REMOTE ENGINEERING

R emote systems like those Todd and Brian work on are fairly new. It's hard to predict what types of technology

Robotic submarines make it possible for people to explore miles below the surface of the ocean.

engineers will be using 20, 30, or 40 years from now. Todd thinks that future arrays will be built that will be able to analyze themselves! If so, these new arrays may not need Todd to help figure out when something is not working properly.

There's no doubt that the future of remote systems is bright. The amount of remote surgery that will be performed is sure to increase. More companies and individuals will use cloud computing to store and protect their information. Drones and other remote technology used in the military will continue to change and improve. Hopefully, we'll continue to explore other planets with rovers and maybe new types of robots that we haven't imagined yet. The key to remote systems in the future will be skilled, well-trained scientists who develop the concepts for new remote systems, and the engineers who build the systems and operate them.

Remote systems will always require skill with computers, and jobs running computer systems are expected to grow in number. The United States Bureau of Labor Statistics predicts that the total number of these jobs will grow faster than many other types of jobs in the coming years. Computer scientist job opportunities will also grow, though maybe not as quickly.

As technology changes, engineers will be the people putting it to work. We will be taking greater advantage of renewable energy sources in the future. There will probably be more wind farms than there are today. Many wind farms are being planned far out in the ocean. You won't be able to see them from a beach. They will have to be operated remotely.

Some scientists work with machines called wave generators that use the power of moving water in the ocean. They work a little like wind towers, but under the water. As waves come in toward the shore, they turn fans. These transform the energy in the water into electrical energy, which is sent to power plants on land. These systems of wave generators are operated remotely and need systems engineers to help them run smoothly.

There may also be more remote systems engineering work carried out in space. In 2009, NASA launched the Kepler space observatory. Kepler's mission is to survey a portion of the Milky Way galaxy to determine if there are other Earthlike planets orbiting stars, the way Earth orbits the Sun. Kepler is controlled by a team of about 35 people who work in a research facility located in Colorado. Every two weeks, the team contacts the space observatory to monitor systems, such as batteries, electricity, and temperatures, and to upload commands. Once a month, the controllers direct the spacecraft to send the data it has collected to NASA's assortment of antennas positioned around the world.

By December 2011, scientists had found 48 objects that may be planets circling stars at just the right distance from the star to support life. Perhaps one of those planets is home to living things.

The mission of the Kepler space observatory is to study an area of about 100,000 stars to search for planets.

How do you think we will explore those planets? Sending rovers is less dangerous and costly than sending humans. Those planets are too far away for a person to survive the trip. In fact, it could take much longer than a person's lifetime to reach them.

It's likely that our first discovery of life on another planet will be accomplished with a remote system. Who will operate that remote system from Earth? A remote systems control engineer, of course!

Will that engineer be you?

LEARNING & INNOVATION SKILLS

Solutions to scientific problems can come from surprising places. Did you know that space travel weakens human bones? A Wisconsin scientist thinks he may have a solution. Joe is a geologist, whose work is to study minerals. But Joe's favorite hobby is hunting for mushrooms in the woods. He has discovered that certain wild mushrooms are packed with vitamins that keep human bones healthy. Joe is working with NASA to better understand how mushrooms can be used to help space travelers. He's also working with a chef on using mushrooms in food for astronauts!

SOME WELL-KNOWN REMOTE SYSTEMS CONTROL ENGINEERS

Alexander Graham Bell (1847–1922) and Charles Sumner Tainter (1854–1940) developed the photophone. It sent audio conversation on light beams. This was the first wireless communications technology and was later used by the military in communications. The photophone also led to the development of some fiber-optic communication methods.

Jean-Daniel Colladon (1802–1893) developed a special tube of water in which he moved sunlight from outside to a lecture table inside. This developed core ideas that led to fiber-optic cable, the fastest and most reliable way to transmit data over long distances. Colladon also showed that sound passes four times faster through water than it does through air.

Brian Cooper (1960–) drove the first Mars rover, *Sojourner*, in 1996. He managed the development of driving controls for the rovers and has operated each Mars rover, including the rover *Curiosity*.

Jacques Marescaux (1948–) led the first remote surgery on September 7, 2001. He performed surgery from New York City on the gallbladder of a 68-year-old woman who was 4,000 miles (6,400 km) away in Strasbourg, France. Doctors in both places communicated by video and personal computers.

GLOSSARY

access (AK-sess) being able to reach or use

animation (an-uh-MAY-shuhn) the activity of making movies by using computer graphics or drawings

arrays (uh-RAYZ) machines that arrange information in an ordered way

cloud computing (KLOUD kuhm-PYOO-ting) the practice of storing regularly used computer data on information storage machines that can be accessed through the Internet

data (DAY-tuh) information collected so that something can be done with it

engineers (en-juh-NEERZ) people who are trained to design and build machines or large structures

hardware (HAHRD-wair) computer equipment, such as a printer, a monitor, or a keyboard

interactive (in-tur-AK-tiv) relating to a form of instruction or entertainment in which people act directly with devices or computer programs

nuclear (NOO-klee-ur) having to do with the energy created from splitting atoms

programs (PROH-gramz) a series of instructions that control the way a computer works

remote systems (ri-MOHT SIS-tuhmz) a group of related or connected things or parts that work together and are controlled by an operator from a distance

software (SAWFT-wair) computer programs that control the workings of the equipment and direct it to do specific tasks

toxic (TAHK-sik) poisonous

FOR MORE INFORMATION

BOOKS

Bortz, Fred. *Seven Wonders of Space Technology.* Minneapolis: Twenty-First Century Books, 2011.

Graham, Ian. *Robot Technology.* Mankato, MN: Smart Apple Media, 2012.

Parker, Steve. *Robots in Dangerous Places.* New York: Franklin Watts, 2011.

WEB SITES

How Stuff Works—How Remote Controls Work
www.howstuffworks.com/remote-control.htm
At this site, you can learn about the history of remote control devices and how they work.

National Aeronautics and Space Administration—The Space Place
http://spaceplace.nasa.gov
Here you'll find information, videos, activities, and games about astronomy and NASA.

Science Kids—Technology for Kids
www.sciencekids.co.nz/technology.html
This site offers fun facts, experiments, games, projects, and videos about many types of science.

INDEX

ABOUT THE AUTHOR

Matt Mullins holds a master's degree in the history of science from the University of Wisconsin–Madison. He writes about all kinds of things, including science and technology, engineering, business, food, and agriculture. Matt has written more than 30 children's books and has made several short films. He lives in Madison, Wisconsin.

The author wishes to thank Todd Assentoa of EMC for his help with this book.